ALSO BY KARL KIRCHWEY

A Wandering Island (1990)

Those I Guard (1993)

THE ENGRAFTED WORD

KARL KIRCHWEY

THE

ENGRAFTED

WORD

POEMS

A *Marian Wood*/Owl Book
Henry Holt and Company   New York

Henry Holt and Company, Inc.
Publishers since 1866
115 West 18th Street
New York, New York 10011

Henry Holt ® is a registered
trademark of Henry Holt and Company, Inc.

Published in Canada by Fitzhenry & Whiteside Ltd.,
195 Allstate Parkway, Markham, Ontario L3R 4T8.

Library of Congress Cataloging-in-Publication Data
Kirchwey, Karl, 1956–
The engrafted word : poems / Karl Kirchwey.—1st ed.
p.   cm.
"A Marian Wood book."
ISBN 0-8050-5607-6 (alk. paper)
I. Title.
PS3561.I684E53 1998   97-28896
811'.54—dc21

The lines in the epigraph from "Thought and Image" by Edwin Muir
are from *Collected Poems*. Copyright © 1965 by E. Muir. Used by
permission of Oxford University Press, Inc.

Henry Holt books are available for special promotions and
premiums. For details contact: Director, Special Markets.

First Owl Books Edition 1998

DESIGNED BY KATE NICHOLS

Printed in the United States of America
All first editions are printed on acid-free paper. ∞

10   9   8   7   6   5   4   3   2   1

THIS BOOK IS FOR TOBIAS

CONTENTS

ACKNOWLEDGMENTS

The poems in this book appeared (sometimes in different forms) in the following periodicals, to whose editors grateful acknowledgment is made:

Antaeus: "Arcadia"
The Colorado Review: "The Gladiators"
The Nation: "Provincetown, February"; "The Wound"; "Milton"
The New Republic: "Sonogram"; "Tiber Island"
The New Yorker: "He Considers the Birds of the Air"; "Zoo Story"; "In Transit"
The Paris Review: "Syracuse"
Partisan Review: "Leaf Season, Columbia County"; "Juno's Song"
Poetry (Chicago): "Barium"
The Southwest Review: "Santa Maria in Trastevere"
TriQuarterly: "Skin Cards"; "Roman Spring"
The Yale Review: "Roman Hours"

"Sonogram" appeared in *Best American Poetry 1995*, Richard Howard, editor; David Lehman, series editor (New York: Scribner, 1995), and also in *The Best of the Best American Poetry*, Harold Bloom, editor; David Lehman, series editor (New York: Scribner, 1998).

"He Considers the Birds of the Air" appeared in *The Gospels in Our Image: An Anthology of Twentieth Century Poetry Based on Biblical Texts*, David Curzon, editor (New York: Harcourt, Brace and Company, 1995).

"Santa Maria in Trastevere" received the Elizabeth Matchett Stover Award for 1996 from *The Southwest Review.*

I would also like to thank the American Academy of Arts and Letters, the American Academy in Rome, the John Simon Guggenheim Memorial Foundation, and the National Endowment for the Arts for grants and fellowships that made available the gift of time.

Wherefore lay apart all filthiness and superfluity
of naughtiness, and receive with meekness the engrafted word,
which is able to save your souls.

—JAMES 1:21

Then braced by iron and by wood,
　　Engrafted on a tree he died,
And little dogs lapped up the blood
　　　That spurted from his broken side.

—EDWIN MUIR

I

SONOGRAM

Something of desk work and pornography,
through succulences of conducting gel.
Vector: creation (in a partial view),

held in the half-dark of the examination room,
just as a wishbone of base mineral
holds pomegranate seed or emerald

or alveolus in a narthex rose.
God's image lies couched safe in blood and matter,
where an ionic snow falls lightly, hushed,

into the deep calm of the body's gulf.
The channel-changer skates . . . tiny hot springs
of the beating heart, or sinuses of thought

like Siracusa's limestone quarries, where
an army of seven thousand starved to death.
The world of line and measure somewhat darkly

honors you in this glass, child: all your hands
will make, all your body will savor,
your mind consider, or your heart regret,

seeking your whole life for such immanence.

BARIUM

Light is time thinking about itself. —Octavio Paz

Here darkness in its proper region
    is brought at last to answer what
light asks of it, the only question
    which counts: has time betrayed you yet?

Outside, it is full midsummer;
    but here the numbers flee across
banked screens and passionlessly shimmer
    like sidewalks under linden trees.

You try not to be here, but elsewhere:
    the sigma-shaped triclinium
of Hadrian's banquets at Tibur,
    splashed with squid ink, and more to come.

Later, you will pass a gallon,
    more or less, of latex enamel,
as blooms of cramp go on and on;
    but now, pitched at a martyr's angle,

naked but still wearing your watch,
    you see the barium blackly move
through trefoil ciliated arch
    of splenic or hepatic curve.

You are become this much of light:
    no use to grieve or to deny.
What shakes you is the appetite
    for life in its complacency,

while, figured on the Axminster,
      are roses, mouths, pyloruses.
Life is so common—but not your
      life. And they are so ravenous.

MILTON

Massachusetts and summer long ago.
    We could not keep our hands off each other.
All one rainy afternoon, I read to you;
    in the deep woods a thrush sang somewhere.

I wept when Adam confesses he cannot live
    without her, alone in the woods again,
so strong the bond of nature; and then Eve
    says life may be sweeter for what she has done.

After you left, I remember feeling as though
    I stood at the edge of a great darkness.
If you and I went back there, I could show
    you just where, in the landscape, I felt this.

But my heart lied, in the extremity of feeling,
    and I knew this too, and for the first time:
that my keeping you somehow lay in my letting
    you go; that I would not die of love like Adam,

who stood there with the fading flower crown
    he wove to celebrate Eve's coming back
from their first separation, petals dropping down,
    and to himself the inward silence broke.

LEAF SEASON, COLUMBIA COUNTY

Down such an avenue of red you came
    three weeks ago today.
Here are the fifty different tints of he-
    moglobin, carelessly

scattered across a muddy country road,
    sufficient, through half-turn,
sacral glissando and pause, to have moved
    the world on its foundation

that fraction which adjusts season and climate
    toward the end of the year.
The sumac and the sugar maple light
    your small face with their color;

the bending road forgets itself in blood.
    O rainy rose-gold prince,
lead us to kindness through the unaltered
    kingdoms of innocence.

HE CONSIDERS THE BIRDS OF THE AIR

(MATTHEW 8:19–20)

We get up at six with him and build a fire.
     Against a choir of straight second-growth woods
     on a morning when the thermometer stands
at zero, he considers the birds of the air.

They hop down and again hop down to the feeder
     beyond the window for the black sunflower seeds
     or the suet's white shoulder, a traffic of chickadees
to which cardinals and pine grosbeaks add color.

His man-in-the-moon face, his eyes of cracked sapphire
     reflect necessity in that repeated
     motion. An infant gazes at some birds,
and for a moment it all balances there,

unblinking, calm, until the slightest feather
     of snow, knocked free by a breeze, drifts toward
     the ground, past curtains hospitably patterned
in red and blue chintz pineapples: mute glitter,

crystal fusillade. He will have nowhere
     to lay his head, no matter how he builds,
     no matter how he watches where unnumbered
small creatures have their being in the weather.

ORTHOPEDICS

A jealous god envied my happiness.
      Your screams, the Hippocratic rise of smoke:
gypsum has soiled the lady doctor's Hermès
      scarf as the saw's teeth whiningly invoke

punishment out of all proportion to
      your innocence. Fixed, those small hoplite thighs,
in a frog crouch—for I did worship you,
      the beauty of those delicate arches

walled up alive, their grace gone masked and numb.
      Stinking moleskin, confected fiberglass
contain you down the weeks of burdened time.
      But I have learned, although my poor statue's

a boy: I have learned cunning, even late,
      and I will guard my love these forty days
till it grows secret, white and pitiless,
      and at last you crack from it like a nut.

ZOO STORY

It *could* have been the soul of my dead mother
I recognized quite accidentally
in the eyes of an Asian elephant cow.
That body shrugged toward me like a boulder
set to run downhill. The trunk idled with a listless
delicacy over dirty straw,
pinkly inquisitive. I heard a sigh.
I do not believe in metempsychosis;
yet, in a temple lobed and domed most strangely,
I mourned again, and worshiped after her,
buried in this landslide of a creature,
its crushing, dreamlike step, its slack repose,
its gaze, deep as the past or the hereafter,
swaying through counts of years, steady on me.

IN TRANSIT

"Sandals more interwoven and complete
To fit the naked foot of poesy. . . ."
I look up, on this now-midmorning ride:
there, angled dozing in a dove-gray seat,
a ginger-haired girl's anonymous beauty
has caught my eye, the usual distraction.
And then, a brick wall on the urban hillside
beyond, sent past at the appropriate
moment in this private itinerary,
is the hospital where my father died.
Forever beyond pity or contrition,
I am fixed, unmoving. I sweat at how
slowly the wheel of my regard moves on.
I will not recall her an hour from now.

II

PROVINCETOWN, FEBRUARY

What are these columns of light
that move between the ocean and the sky?

Out there where there is no one until the Azores,
the dust of a djinn is passing,

or the rumor of a city's desolation
on the other side of the world:

nothing but the wind-borne fume of sea salt, of iodine,
riding dolphin-back across the bottle-green prairies

of unloved space with a retrograde holler.
Traveler chased by sand, the hurt of this cold

is like the exile's last glimpse of home, a low coast
bruised by the light of afternoon, hardly resisting

the ocean's passage from nowhere to nowhere, ligamented
to the sky itself with bands of inhuman force.

CHILDLESSNESS

Cruor of Aphrodite. S.A. labs.
      Dreams of motility. The bridegroom wakes
      and then the bride. Bound overhead from LAX
screaming through the republic's outworn hubs,

the redeye loses height at 7:03
      for Pelham (where "sainted Anne Hutchinson"
      lived on the marsh and died of Indians)
and the long turn toward LaGuardia.

Morning comes up, a bickering of sparrows
      in the bare ivy runners and a whiff
      of kerosene blown from the east. And if
the winter drives into them, croup and claws,

where shall they find their warmth? John Winthrop said,
      when Mistress Hutchinson miscarried, that
      the botched fetus brought too early to light
"was twenty-seven several lumps of man's seed

without mixture of anything from the woman,"
      by which he meant the monster of her body
      proceeded from her mind's monstrosity,
to think Christ's righteousness should not find in

her something of an answering righteousness,
      amid the high percent of primitive
      forms in imagination. So forgive
them if their faith should laugh outright at this,

an angel hammered in titanium
       which slams down and rolls shuddering to a halt,
       glinting in clotted light. They cannot salt
this witching cloak of ice. O kingdom come.

RAPTURE

Wetting a forefinger, the winter breeze
    turns the pages of a sodden magazine
abandoned on a bench. Like a scarf from a purse,
    one woman opens another and draws her on.

A hawk sits in the top of a tree nearby,
    with huge pale yellow eyes, turning its head,
then pushes off. The branch swings convulsively,
    freed of that weight, its chunky buteo glide.

One morning I found the wings of a white dove
    intact on the pavement with nothing in between,
just the bloody tendons of consuming love,
    the body shed at last, and imagination

having succeeded in taking flight somewhere.
    After a while their positions have changed.
One woman is licking the fingers of another,
    and neither is wearing a scarf. The breeze has arranged

all this in the intervals of pale sunlight.
    What occupies that flightless space naturally?
A gaze, unblinking in the melting quiet.
    Such are the prompts of appetite in February.

TIBER ISLAND

IN MEMORIAM AMY CLAMPITT

The Tiber muddles by,
     stroking its beard of filthy weed.
     The harbor police have been rusticated;
their rubber boat is dry.

On the stone overhead,
     inscriptions obscured by wild fig
     proclaim four times: This is the bridge
Lucius Fabricius made,

and a homeless man in a box
     once belonging to some appliance
     reads a magazine and reclines
as if at a banquet. A dog barks

at him and at the tedium
     from a balcony,
     running back and forth, hard to see
behind the leggy geranium,

while below the rapids, a pleasure boat,
     like a fat lady stranded on an Imperial stair,
     waits for fall rains to lift her over,
winched up with a hook in the throat.

An edge of travertine
     visible in a foundation wall
     still bears the unrobed, capable
shoulders and the Epidaurian

serpent wound on its staff.
>   But the god's face has been sheared away.
>   Little boat, *Isola Tiberina*,
still at large on these waters after

so long, we are simply too late.
>   He doesn't come anymore, to touch
>   the hopeful in the sleeping porch,
telling this one to eat

pine cones and honey
>   on a regimen of three days
>   for hemorrhage, or ashes
and wine in a poultice for pleurisy,

or the blood of a white cockerel
>   and honey for the sight of the blind,
>   or the five fingers of one hand
placed on the altar, then on the eyes as well.

We are too late; we know too much.
>   In this place of refuge and exile,
>   we are quarantined. There will
be no miracle, not with our knowledge,

and, bound upriver, a crane
>   seems barely to graze
>   the sullen eddies in places:
gone; gone; gone; gone.

ROMAN HOURS

1. THE HOROLOGIUM OF AUGUSTUS
(13 B.C.)

We
are led into
a courtyard off Via di Campo
Marzio #48, past a man in a little shop

who
is fixing shoes,
down to the basement and across a
sort of catwalk to a shaky ladder, at the foot of which we

see,
through a meter
of standing water, the bronze letters
set in travertine which say Ε Τ Η Σ Ι Α Ι Π Α Υ Ο Ν Τ Α Ι, that is

"The
Etesian winds
stop," as they do on the Aegean
at the end of summer, when the sun is in Virgo. It was a

dream
of emperors,
teaching even the sun at last to
walk orderly between monuments and anniversaries which

are
the expression
of a self both invisible and
immortal, one identical with the world of natural law,

now
beyond the griefs
of cracked and linear time, ablaze
in the incised tangle of the analemma, being rather

part
of time itself,
untouchable, having transcended
dynastic art, a shadow walking between the Mausoleum

of
Augustus and
the Ara Pacis, on whose threshold
there stood, on the Emperor's birthday, this solar affirmation

that
the past, given
the pattern of the divine, had been
made present; that the future, being certain, was also present.

Deep
beneath modern
pavements, the pinched grace of these lines still
remembers the moment the wind's breath died on the water's face; the

shade,
the touch of it,
cast by a human head lost in thought,
to whom it occurred that the one way to godhead was through absence.

2. THE MERIDIAN OF SANTA MARIA DEGLI ANGELI

(A.D. 1703)

A crumb of light
high on the southern wall
of a pagan frigidarium
supposedly built by Christian slaves
under the Emperor Diocletian
(but there were ways out
to forswear libel flee profane)
and now become a church

That pure ellipsis trembles
by which one thing becomes another
moving leisurely in a double focus
across the marble inlay of a floor
wrought with signs of the zodiac
Clouds swim across
as it lights the hooves of an amiable ram
done in *giallo antico*

In the heavens as on earth
what is taken for observed truth
is not quite the same thing as law
The historian writes *As the lives*
of the faithful became
less mortified and austere
they were every day less ambitious
of the honors of martyrdom

Beyond the heliacal hole
is the ineffable core
toward which the motes climb and climb

A few people wait far below
impatiently as if knowing
they must respect this motion
but no longer knowing quite why
and at 12:17:45 exactly

by my watch (legal time not solar time)
the macula crosses the bronze rail
it walks between Resurrection and Resurrection
silent traveler considering one by one
the sequence of letters
TERMINUS PASCHAE
considering the disordered world
humans have made of paradise

3. The Janiculum Cannon

(A.D. 1847)

It was Pius IX who decided
    that the bark of a howitzer should
replace the exuberant riot
    of the city's church bells, their uncoordinated

ringing, and therefore establish
    the hour of noon for the rabble.
The shakoed soldiers push
    the monster from its cave in the hill,

count backward in Italian,
    and the crowd flinches and recognizes
once again the voice of extinction
    by which it may tell the hours.

At the puppet theater nearby, Pulcinella
    is beaten around the head with a stick
by the Devil for the third time today.
    The children are silent and do not blink.

The cannon was elsewhere during
    the period of the Second World War,
the population finding
    other ways to fill its appetite for gunpowder;

nor again until 1959
    (lest the custom seem precocious,
or the dead too soon forgotten)
    did that stroke of outrageous noise

strip the tender green from each branch
      and announce its message to all
in accents of intolerant bronze.
      Through the smoke in its acrid blue coil,

we thank you, Pápa, we thank you,
      who taught us to make the sky
way over by the Pincio
      clap its hands in reply.

III

JUNO'S SONG

1.

Today in the garden,
a peacock spread his tail,
    sprung rake of whalebone
corset stays, balding scribble

    of lapis lazuli.
Across the granite curb,
    preposterous beauty
began once more to absorb

    itself in itself,
swayed by and hoisted
    its tent above
your small gold head,

    and *amour-propre*
opened its slow fan,
    defying the air
for a count of ten.

    In the arrogant quiet,
that screen of aqua
    played with the fright
and the rapture

    in your eyes, then shivered,
poplar-fashion,
    and indolently folded
its starry vanes.

2.

Child, how shall I teach
    your hundred eyes to sleep,
        in which the bird is figured
            as on an engraved gem
        or a Christian tomb,
    its flesh through centuries
thought incorruptible?

Still they blink and watch!
    Is it the scream of peacocks
        through palm and ancient ilex
            by which you are pursued,
        through the complicated air
    and smell of oleander,
the yell and mew of longing,

into the lapis tabernacle
    of your oblivion?
        Now they begin to droop
            deliciously and swim,
        as mundane emerald
    contrives to fan the brow
where sleep is building now.

AMALFI

The smell of a fig tree
      conjures sexual readiness
            in the hot light of afternoon.
            The leaves of the abutilon
are flecked with sun and shadowy
      above a terra-cotta vase

and tremble with the plaintive
      cries of cats, the wail
            of peacocks or stifled
agitation of doves
            through hours jalousied
      and close, while

lemons ride pendulous,
      lamplike, heavy,
            noctilucent
in perfumed arbors
            fogged with salt,
      in ravines plunging to the sea,

and discords of metal
      ring the hour
            and then, a minor third below,
      the quarter,
as if on reliquary skulls
            of Diomede or Basilio,

Eastern saints
    translated here,
       and tolling back
through capital innocence
    those who will never
       feel the hieratic

mysteries advance,
    except as each sense begs
       down dappled pergolas to
quench the light of lemons
    and through
    the body, hush the loud smell of figs.

ARCADIA

As for Arcadia—I can tell you, I lived there for a while—
and whatever its advantages for children,
it's the kind of place you would have been in a hurry
to get out of if you'd gotten any older there.

It's true that back then you could still swim in the lake.
Water slipped over the dam in a coppery braid
with a brackish smell or waited behind the spillway,
filtering daylight through tannin like a sepia print.

In winter, your older brother skated so gracefully
over the polished ice in the last light of dusk
(and he was still years away from yogic flying)
as you lay spread-eagled, face-down in your snowsuit,

studying the lower world like a darkened room.
Behind that small island was a region of particular mystery,
best explored, summer mornings, in a flat-bottomed boat
belonging to your closest friend, a girl with red hair.

By now she is a musician living in Germany.
Her parents are both dead, and somebody else
younger than you are has just lost his wife.
Your own father, for that matter—almost his last words

concerned the school vacation dates in Arcadia.
But even to mention these details is somehow misleading,
for things do not ever change in Arcadia.
It was you who left on that morning thirty years ago,

after all, hardly knowing that you would revisit this landscape
for the rest of your life in dreams, until the events
of sleep and those of childhood became nearly indistinguishable.
Do you want to know the real reason you can't go back?

Not just because loss has touched you and everyone you know,
or because Arcadia is the place you know before loss.
But here you were feeling everything for the first time,
and particular emotion arose like a genius of place,

whether solitude, or being on the mend from illness,
or hurrying through a pine forest to get someplace else,
where you waited, in the end, for something enormous
to happen, and of course it did, and you grew up.

SYRACUSE

If you're thinking of going to Syracuse,
    be modest and do not expect
the bronze warriors of Reggio
    to blink at the prospect
with their limestone eyes,
or to whistle high-low
    through their silver teeth.
    There will be no one to go with,
because you decided suddenly
    on this trip. Friends won't change their plans.
Are you sure you won't be lonely?
    It often happens.

If you are still determined,
    remember that the Pensione Edelweiss
in Taormina won't give you a room
    for one night, even if there's space.
They will be insistent and bland
and sympathetic. You will hate them,
    as you climb back into your small
    underpowered vehicle.
Others will crowd, flash and swerve,
    pass you with a curse and a gesture
on a hill, in a tunnel, on a curve
    of a highway which is there and not there.

When you get to Catania,
    lava-cobbled and lava-corniced,
it will feel like a city in Hell.

You will water the stones with your sweat
on a day of thick haze and humidity,
and Etna permanently invisible.
        Birds in cages and an idiot child singing
        will keep you awake all night long,
and though this is only a place
        on the way to your true destination,
you may feel, red-eyed and morose,
        discommoded and tense, that it is an omen.

At last you will arrive
        in the fabled city and find it dying,
sister, in its day, to Athens,
        swans and fish sluggish among
papyrus where Arethusa the nymph
once fled Alpheus; and the idea that the fountain's
        waters and the ocean's never mix
        is a fabulation of ancient hydraulics,
you will conclude, as you sit
        before a *granita di limone* in the square
when the waiter has fiercely knit
        his brows at your accent and your order.

And the disillusionment won't stop there.
        You won't get in to see *The Burial of Saint Lucy*—
in fact, no one will even tell you where she is.
        You will shuttle about looking ludicrously
for that throat, hacked as if by a serial killer,
then toned down. Truth will rise to the surface
        in your mind like a pentimento
        in the late work of Caravaggio.

Two brutes with their gleaming shovels
        in a slurry of shit-colored light
are digging a grave for your travels.
        Of course you won't like it.

In this place that knows no day without sun,
        you may begin to feel quite dark.
You may feel you are being laughed at
        by the little contorted terra-cotta
temple antefix of a gorgon
face which you recently bought;
        and as for beauty, the citrus
        orchards, green in limestone quarries,
don't remember the bones of the army
        which perished there of exposure
because of hubris and treachery,
        so this shouldn't trouble you, either.

You may feel that life is all irony,
        Plato sold in the market for a slave
by a tyrant, the elder Dionysius;
        but really he ought not to have
come to Syracuse, so convinced was he
of the superiority of ideas to practice.
        But you don't have that problem—
        or at least you won't by the time
you depart, if, after all,
        you do. You won't be wrong to go
to Syracuse, that city of fable.
        Remember you were warned, though.

THE HOUR OF PRAISE

A cast-iron cornice beetling with swags
    blackly preponderates across the street.
Shuffling forward on phlebitic legs
    toward a window thrown open for the heat,

a figure appears in a gray chemise,
    whether man or woman impossible to tell,
wrinkled, with close-cropped hair and vacant eyes,
    to take a place in this Imperial

facade. The keystone bears a lion's head,
    snarling at the entrenched humidity.
The windowsill is heavily meandered.
    Posed on both elbows now, methodically

this citizen pares the skin off a ripe peach
    in one downy and sweetly bleeding ribbon.
The darkened room yawns just behind, through which
    a breeze dies. (There's a cyclospora scare on.)

The world shrugs on its spindle, wearied by
    such perturbations of the late Antique;
and yet requiring, in its hard bounty,
    the presence of those whom it most implac-

ably ignores, their stifled, gravid watching,
    as if of cattle brought to sacrifice
and met at last with the hammer-bearing
    god Charun's black grin at the hour of praise.

IV

SKIN CARDS

Pliny tells how a man once fell in love
    with Praxiteles' Cnidean Venus.
      He visited her at night, and his embrace
left stains on the marble where the thighs cleave.

O perfumed brink, sweet pelt, world's predicate,
    forgetful verb, to your one agile place
      the dark tends, sunset-edged, regret's deep fosse
through myth and all the centuries of heat.

TWO FOR THE EMPEROR TIBERIUS

1.TENCH

A scorched saffron reticule
containing the week's stale bread
(the blackened crust tastes slightly bitter)
makes a yawp and a tambourine swirl
in the water, then softens, grows morbid,
mouthing syllables of air;

and a frosted stocking is smirched with charcoal
in some exploit when the gates
have closed, a sweet buss and thrash where
drifting milt knits to vermeil
in muscular elaborations that wet
the glad hand of the beholder;

or even gaudier missteps of the gene pool:
a fisherman once surprised Tiberius
on his rugged island of pleasure;
there is blood in the crisscross of scales
where the guards used the gift of the poor
man to rub the skin off his face.

Beauty and malignant shame mingle
in a fry of albino gold
and whiskered calico. Witness this hunger,
flamboyant and utterly normal,
as their poached blindnesses suck the mud
and bask in the sun with a dull glitter.

2. GANYMEDE

FOR MARK AESCHLIMAN

Tiberius has had a statue
of the Phrygian shepherd boy
carved in a rare skunked marble
mixing soil and purity
to crown his cave at Sperlonga,

its banqueting dais surrounded
entirely by water
and scenes carved from *The Odyssey*
(the blinding of Polyphemus)
as the winter sun is quenched

in the Tyrrhenian Sea,
and the tide wanders in and out
among terra-cotta jars set
in the piers of marine cement
to make a fish hatchery,

the settled economy of purpose
and practical ingenuity
surviving the chaos of emotion.
But the heart of the Emperor is old,
perverse and old, tired of humanity.

It fills him with restlessness
and spiders him over with regret:
the thing he loved best was broken.
That face, beaded with water,
hair sleeked like an otter's in the spin

of reflections off veined stone,
seems to mock his crooked patience
with its no more than radiance of flesh.
In the reluctance of his power,
he sees again like an adversary

the beauty which he has had killed
and made an ornament of the Empire,
given up to that which he despises
for not knowing how it would end:
the thunder's descent from the roof.

Rebuked by such unselfconsciousness,
he is tender above the translucent nape.
Then a blow, a backwash to crouch in,
and the frantic pedaling
of naked legs down the cliff.

THE GLADIATORS

(VILLA BORGHESE MOSAICS, FOURTH CENTURY A.D.)

ALUMNUS has just killed MAZICINUS
    with a dagger or short sword.
He's standing on his head, MAZICINUS,
    soaking the sand with his blood

—but it was too late for views to be correct.
    The workmanship is coarse;
beauty is gone; there is only effect.
    Stain heightens the stones' colors.

Nearby, CALLIMORFUS is dying too,
    with a sucking wound in his chest,
while SERPENTIUS, braced, slopes his lance into
    a vaulting spotted beast,

and blood sluices down in a thick red flag.
    TALAMONIUS has just killed
trident-man AURIUS, with a big
    Θ beside his name, whose pallid

unlucky face is pillowed on his arm
    as if he were taking a nap
in the middle of the roaring stadium.
    AURIUS will not wake up.

What was it like to live in a failing empire?
    Constant changes, always hard,
and with them never the peace one had hoped for,
    and no one really prospered,

except in proving Rome's old gods were gone,
        each violent epitome
revealed in misstep and unguarded motion
        as mere fatality.

BELLEREFONS kneels over CUPIDO and has
        plunged, or will soon, a dagger
into his throat: another Θ for *Thanatos*.
        It may have been MELEAGER

who killed AURIUS, language faltering
        before the crisis of a narrative
in which one more named—nicknamed—human being
        takes the big cartoon dive

to die—and die: the handsome LICENTIOSUS,
        who "heals girls in the night,"
who is their "boss," kills someone who is nameless;
        however, those girls will not

remember him when, in his turn, he falls.
        MELIIIO, having gathered
a straight lance from his name's redundant vowels,
        breaks it off in a leopard.

A slave is brandishing a rawhide quirt:
        IACULATOR, under blows,
has killed RODAN (Θ), not born to it,
        but an adept at slaughter nonetheless,

caught up in the work of one afternoon.
        Nothing in nature is as cruel as these,
violence unlimbering in silence on
        ruined recovered floors,

the property of citizens to whom
    it must have given momentary comfort—
their keeping, in suburban polychrome,
    death always underfoot.

TWO LANDSCAPES IN NUMIDIA

1. *GIALLO ANTICO*

(SIMITTHUS, TUNISIA)

Peace sleeps in the green valley now.
The aqueduct's piers stagger from nowhere to nowhere,
and the muddy river swells past one remaining bridge arch,

its keystone, like affliction, still in place.
It is necessary to imagine a world in which nature itself
has been traduced, and participates in oppression—

the Mejerda, for example, which once powered the mill
which ground the grain which fed the slaves who quarried the marble
and worked it, sometimes until they died:

Puteolamus, Corinthus, Callistus, Felix,
to mention a few whose names were written down.
The red tape stretched all the way from here to Carthage,

and the system, it was thought, in its mechanical ingenuity,
might reasonably last forever.
Human extremities seen with the light behind them

glow with something of this veined warmth, or the evening cloud
on the road to Teboursook, which so much resembled
the skinned carcass of a goat hung in a tile doorway,

a pink star hung in the faultless blue of dusk.
A German scholar has just published splendid isometric drawings
of what, inevitably, he calls the *Lager,*

with its long rows of sleeping benches and latrines,
the whole thing discreetly separated from the Roman town
by the bulk of the quarry itself, a gouged-out hillside

where the rose-gold scree still slips around your ankles
with an iron music, and your shouts are swallowed whole.
There is talk of starting the quarry up again,

an inexhaustible supply, and the only one in the world.
Perhaps it is true that the pathology of a civilization
may be read in its love, its quite inordinate love,

of this rare and difficult stone, worked stone, *marmor numidicum.*
Perhaps it was even worth it, if your tastes run to this kind of marble,
which after all they may not.

2. THE ROMAN QUARRIES AT GHAR EL KEBIR

Our somewhat intense and self-appointed cicerone
is a young Tunisian man in need of money.

At that hour when the bat, *twir-el-lil*,
is a nervousness at the edge of the visible,

he materializes out of the blowing dusk.
What language is it that we speak, he asks.

We follow him obediently into the caves.
He is eager to develop a theory: that the slaves

spent their entire lives down in this place.
The conviction of it, and one flashlight, shine in his face.

That pit choked with rubble was the punishment cell;
here is a wretched oven, and there is a well.

Here is where they slept, and there is where they slept for good.
It opens overhead in a negative pyramid

of surmises. The humanists among us don't see the point,
arguing that neither logic nor economics would warrant

such a closed system, the sky a hole forty feet up
through which the blocks were hauled with groaning ropes.

Someone asks, What was the philosopher pony's
name, in Zola? Our guide drops to his knees

before a plant whose dull and wrinkled crown
of leaves seems unremarkable. Forked human,

poor shrieking root, he speaks. We stumble up
to our mild privileges (food, love, sleep),

to night itself, grown indistinguishable
from that other darkness. Tomorrow we will

see quarried blocks from here in the foundation
of the Antonine Baths in Carthage, also in ruin;

but first our own day must have its ending.
Bataille. Mandragora. They all died for nothing.

V

ROMAN SPRING

The wow of zinc hoardings in the *tramontana*
    with naked bodies on them (a cellulite pill)
(Hope they don't catch cold in this lapidary weather);
    artichokes and underwear in each market stall;

rain-soaked brickwork, and a stained mattress
    abandoned in a field of trampled crim-
son poppies; jasmine and excrement; flowering capers;
    the salt sea smell behind the smell of petroleum;

the first strawberries, in from Terracina,
    where the Romans built Jove Anxur a temple
on arcades which seem to retreat forever
    into the middle distance of pure will;

the warble of a police walkie-talkie
    outside the home of the Vatican ambassador (who
is an ex-mayor of Boston), incongruously
    reminiscent of a thrush in the Massachusetts woods long ago;

that moment, early on a foggy morning,
    When the domes of all the city's churches press
upward like the bubble of aspiration in a running
    prayer from the plain that once kept Romulus;

and a travertine curb polished like something priceless
    by the bus's slow turn as it grinds uphill;
the strong grip of those packed and swaying riders
    as they are carried through the Papal Wall.

TWELVE EPIGRAMS FOR
PASSION WEEK, ISCHIA

1.
The island dogs run free and crap on the beach
among the used syringes and empty bottles of bleach.

2.
The sea has also tossed up bracelets of Jaffa grapefruit.
Kennst du das Land, a transistor sings out.

3.
From the radio mast of the *Pellicano III*
has sprung the living branch of an olive tree.

4.
They have come to worship the beardless Christ, Apollo, *Sol Invictus*,
a people sober, near the millennium, and prosperous.

5.
This white breast stained with rose, patient, withstood
the familiar access of catamenial blood.

6.
They wrap their new potatoes in a hotel towel
and bury them in the sands, which are geothermal.

7.
An Alsatian hunches into the offshore breeze
and trembles, in the attitude of all sufferers.

8.

The Judas tree pegs up its vernal gore,
indifferent if Easter should fall on Passover.

9.

The whole place hisses softly, fit to explode.
The light is blond above a mask of mud.

10.

This morning a file cabinet washed in from the sea,
battered metal, jonquil yellow. It was empty.

11.

Emotion lingers, sub-hysterical:
hyssop, bruised head, vinegar mixed with gall.

12.

They flee in hectic wraiths, rags of live steam
torn from the piled rocks which first conceived them.

VILLANELLE

This tree's not like the one they slew Him on.
We are cutting out a slender cardboard T.
They broke the legs of the first and the other one.

The green wood of your leg, like theirs, is broken.
A tree for spring to decorate, maybe:
this tree's not like the one they slew Him on.

We say the alphabet, lingering when
we reach the fatal letter of that tree.
They broke the legs of the first and the other one,

and they became different letters then,
as mercy can be parsed from misery.
This tree's not like the one they slew Him on:

its beams are warped to **P**; in canceled motion,
they slip and fold, becoming merely **X**.
They broke the legs of the first and the other one.

One day your body will be whole again,
but now it is a heavy, swaying toy.
This tree's not like the one they slew Him on.
They broke the legs of the first and the other one.

THE WOUND

(VERROCCHIO'S *CHRIST AND SAINT THOMAS*)

You have indeed chosen a dark place, Thomas,
    this letter slot, this closing kitchen drawer,
        in which to catch your hand.
        How can you understand,
    glass-gazer that you are, smooth-faced time server,
so amiable and expressionless,

that to be merely present is not what
    was ever required of you? Let exile sharpen
        these words, then, like a lance blade
        chased with ivy, inscribed
    by some doxy to her departing Roman,
"Come back alive. Come back hugely in rut."

In the dust of Mylapore or Parthia,
    you will remember how the shocking pink
        widened like a sunrise,
        giving onto the grievous
    truth just beneath, the bubbling rebuke
across the intercostal ivory.

Your face reflected, through its sheeplike curls,
    upon that last hour, when the common daylight
        in its crosscutting beams
        arrived from many kingdoms
    and for a moment seemed to mitigate
the darkness falling. Still the darkness falls.

You think somehow that Asiatic face,
      its half-smile mandarin with suffering,
          composes itself to speak.
          But this is your mistake,
      now with the image as once with the living
Word, incapable still to realize,

for all you have seen, all you have imagined,
      the nature of the gift. Finally, with
          your ignorance of Him,
          how could He not become
      thin-lipped with weird anger? Because, in truth,
mine was the only voice to which you listened.

SANTA MARIA IN TRASTEVERE

Into this gilded space, my only son,
  we wander on most Saturdays, to light
a votive candle for this one or that one
  you will never know, and to admire the granite

columns great labor once brought to the Nile
  across the desert, a distance of sixty
miles, pleasing Roman eyes with their dense sparkle
  of star-shot night, their depth of galaxy,

especially after rain, being swagged with red
  wandering garlands of fire through pepper-and-salt,
worlds behind worlds, and throughout something livid.
  The legend goes that Heracles nursed at

the breast so hard milk spurted in an arc
  into the Milky Way; but over time,
it seems myth always hardens into work.
  A.D. 118, and a transport team

sent, on papyrus, this correspondence:
  an urgent request for supplies of barley;
a fifty-foot shaft weighing ninety tons
  stalled in the cursing sands of Jebel Fatireh.

No other word. And now their pagan strength
  supports an arduous glistening of old
mosaics in a Christian arch of triumph,
  scenes from the Virgin's life, a life not made

in fear and pleasure as your life has been.
　　　My prayer, given the vanity of all
the work this world has so abounded in,
　　　　　is that the necessary and beautiful

should draw your soul, unbaptized and still bright,
　　　through its exhaustion: as, through one whole day,
oil in this place, in a miraculous fount,
　　　　　ran with a clear and modest fluency.

IN THE MUSEUM AT TIVOLI

Here is a chunk of the cornice
        from the Temple of Hercules Victor,
with carved rosettes and acanthus
        from 100 B.C. at Tibur.
                First the place was an iron foundry,
        and then it made red butcher paper
                from wheat stalks and ordinary hay.

A spirit of organized labor,
        therefore, seems to inhabit
the empty vaults, whether a god or
        just the proletariat.
                The Anio's loud cascade,
        rich in calcium carbonate,
                over time created

this piece of travertine,
        which was quarried nearby
and hoisted up to crown
        the edifice gracefully,
                until, in the course of time,
        it fell, and once more lay
                on the river bottom.

First nature's, it became
        man's, then once more nature's.
The gradual skills of lime-
        stone worked each swollen rose
                back to its primeval
        form, making thick with calculus
                each sharp-edged dentil,

until one day a human
            eye saw, through the clear water,
the burled lump and accretion
            and understood them for
                        the integuments of a flowering
            too old to remember,
                        a lost and twice-made thing.

How does the children's game go?
            Scissors cut the paper
I write upon, although
            by stone, in turn, they are
                        blunted, and paper wraps
            stone brought to architecture.
                        And here, for now, it stops.

NOTES

"Sonogram": "Siracusa's limestone quarries" refers to an open-air prison for the Athenians, defeated in 413 B.C., as described in Thucydides.

"Milton": the last line quotes Milton's *Paradise Lost*, IX.895.

"Orthopedics": the first line paraphrases a tag in Greek drama; for example, Euripides, *Alcestis* 1135.

"In Transit": the lines quoted are from a sonnet by Keats.

"Childlessness": "S.A. labs" refers to semen analysis. "Sainted Anne Hutchinson" is Hawthorne's ironic phrase in *The Scarlet Letter*. The passage quoted is from the journal of John Winthrop (1588–1649), first governor of the Massachusetts Bay Colony.

"Tiber Island": "the unrobed, capable/ shoulders" are those of a sculptural fragment depicting Aesculapius, the Greek god of healing, whose temple stood on the island.

"The Horologium of Augustus": this poem imitates, in a syllabic stanza form, the series of mathematical squares constituting the gnomon, which we also know as the pointer on a sundial.

"The Meridian of Santa Maria degli Angeli": the italicized lines are from Edward Gibbon's *Decline and Fall of the Roman Empire*.

"The Roman Quarries at Ghar El Kebir": "They all died for nothing" echoes a passage in Clive James's essay "Blaming the Germans" in *The New Yorker*, 22 April 1996.

"Twelve Epigrams for Passion Week, Ischia": "*Kennst du das Land*" is from the Goethe poem in *Wilhelm Meister*, as set by many composers. The cult of Sol Invictus flourished, particularly in the Roman army, during the first centuries of Christianity.

"Villanelle": the Greek letters are pronounced *rho* and *chi*, respectively.

"Santa Maria in Trastevere": the stone described, originally quarried in the Red Sea mountains of Egypt, is *Mons claudianus* granite.